Living with a Portuguese Water Dog

Living with a Portuguese Water Dog

A Love-Hate relationship

Sylvia Mennear

Copyright © 2009 by Sylvia Mennear.

Library of Congress Control Number: 2009912689
ISBN: Hardcover   978-1-4500-0687-3
              Softcover   978-1-4500-0686-6
              Ebook   978-1-4500-0688-0

All rights reserved. No part of this book may be reproduced or transmitted in any form or by any means, electronic or mechanical, including photocopying, recording, or by any information storage and retrieval system, without permission in writing from the copyright owner.

This book was printed in the United States of America.

To order additional copies of this book, contact:
Xlibris Corporation
1-888-795-4274
www.Xlibris.com
Orders@Xlibris.com
72529

Contents

Purchasing Our Dog 11
Jim's New Work Partner 16
More than just a dog 19
A Brief History and profile of the breed 21
I Don't Like His "I Think I'm King Behavior" 26
My First Birthday Party 29
My First Christmas Alone 30
Another member to our family 32
Holidays With Or Without Him 36
Visits From Oma 41
Barney's Last Chapter 44
Our last weekend with barney 46
Life after Barney 52
Our 2nd Generation Kids 53
Our Puppy Is A Monster 60
Theo's New Friend 63
Theo Needs A Live-In Companion 68
Theo And His Shadow 71
It Feels Like we have 2 toddlers in the house 75
Princessa Comes Home 78
Princessa Is Going To Be A Momma 81
Eight Dogs in the house 84
Our 2nd Generation Kids 85
Acknowledgements 91

*This Book is dedicated
In
Loving Memory of Barney*

We miss you!

This novel is based on the life and times with our beloved Barney—Portuguese Water Dog

And then in later years our (2nd Generation kids) 4 spoiled dogs, Theodore, Shadow, Princessa and Ozzie who become a little family.

Purchasing Our Dog

Picture Perfect

When purchasing a dog, it is reasonable to say that you should do research on the breed that you are going to purchase. The last thing you want to do is have a dog that you know nothing about, their quirks, allergies, and their hereditary problems. What their life span is, whether or not they would be good around kids, good watchdog, depending of course on what you want a dog for, can you handle the young growing years of a dog? i.e. the puppy stage.

Well we were one of those families that knew nothing about the dog that we were about to purchase. I just wanted a small dog, which this one wasn't going to be, unbenounced to me. It was the right time, my son was around 5 years old and we thought it would be a good time to add a dog to the family.

We couldn't afford to spend much money, so we knew that it wasn't going to be a purebred. We searched the papers every week for anything that sounded interesting. I knew I wanted a small dog, the last thing I wanted to do was pick up large size dog doodies in the back yard and have a large slobbering dog in the house. I also knew that he/she would be a house dog so it would have to be a clean dog.

We finally found an ad that sounded interesting; it read: **"9 puppies, small build and adorable for sale $25.00, ready to go in 1 week"**, the price was right. So we had made an appointment to go visit the dogs. We were brought to the basement of the house and there they were 9 pups and the mom. The mom came to greet us right away, she was small, I would guestamate around 25 lbs. and she was white with streaks of grey. She was about the right size for me and she was friendly and very attentive of her pups. There were so many to choose from we didn't know how to choose a pup, for this was our first family dog. So we played with them for a while. There was one in particular that stood out amongst them all, "he" was the only one that kept coming to us. After we had played with them all and they went about their own business, this particular one would stay; it was like he was saying "I'm the one you're going to take home". Well guess what, . . . we took him. So we put a reserve on him and picked him up in a week when he was ready to come home.

That was the last week of sanity in our house, but even if we knew how our lives would be changed we probably would have still gone forward with buying a dog, because no matter how much grief, misery and destruction he gave us. He gave us so much more happiness and love in the long term. We never knew we could love an animal as much as we loved Barney. Even our families loved him as if he were theirs. In reality, he really was the family dog.

We decided to name him Barney; it was the perfect name for a dog. Our son also had the purple stuffed Barney teddy, so it was just fitting. Barney was a very curious dog, he had to check everything out whether it belonged to him or not. I left a necklace on the coffee table one day, I couldn't find where it had gone, I traced back my steps, my husband and son helped me look for it, to no avail. I ended up finding it in with the dogs' toys. Even when cleaning up his messes in the yard we would find chewed up toys, or pieces of things that we knew were not supposed to be there. Even rope, can you believe that? So we had to be careful as to where we left things, because Barney assumed everything belonged in his mouth. Even as he matured, pulling items out of his mouth was an ongoing thing.

In later years when we moved to the Interior, there was a property behind us approximately 5 acres with a few horses on it. When Barney escaped the yard he headed straight to that property and ate as much dried horse poop as he could find, occasionally he brought some home . . . for a little snack later.

Barney wouldn't give up anything

The first couple of days were extremely hard on us. We both worked full-time, so there would be no one at home to take care of him. We didn't have anywhere that we could lock him up. The laundry room was downstairs and there weren't any windows in that room so we didn't feel right leaving him in this room while we were out. So we gave him the run of the house. **Wrong, Wrong**, never leave a puppy the run of the house. He pooped everywhere, ate whatever he wanted, including chewing up toys that weren't his. So when I got home from work I had an awful mess to clean up, not what I was looking forward to doing before preparing dinner. The second day was worse; he pulled the cushions off the couch and dug holes into the couch, so the springs were showing through. There was stuffing all over the place. He had even pooped on the couch. When I came home that day I screamed, I could have killed him. I was fed up and realized that I didn't want a dog anymore we just couldn't keep him, he was destroying our home, and it wasn't fair to him to be alone all day. So when my husband came home we discussed it and decided the next day being a Saturday Jim would bring Barney to the SPCA. I hated the thought, but I knew someone would take him because he was still a puppy. I just couldn't deal with him anymore, and we weren't attached to him yet.

So the next day came and we said our goodbye's to Barney and watched out the window as Jim put him in the car and drove away. I was not feeling very good about what I asked Jim to do, I was actually very sad and had tears in my eyes. My son was worried that no one would take him, but I told him not to worry someone will take him, hopefully someone that can stay at home with him and has a large area for him to run around. Well Jim hadn't come home for a few hours, and during this time I was really feeling awful about giving him away, I really missed him, I thought maybe we just didn't give him enough time. But did I want to take the chance of having the house destroyed even more. So when Jim got home he said it really hurt him to take Barney to the pound and asked the caretaker what the chances were of someone picking him up. He told him not to worry chances were in his favor because he was young. The last thing we would want was for them to put him to sleep because no one wanted him. That ate at me through the night, it bothered Jim too, the . . . what if no one wanted him, what would happen?

He was a beautiful dog, and he was very young still, and we really didn't have much experience with a dog. We both had dogs growing up, but they weren't our responsibility, I mean we were just kids. Well we never spoke of it much that evening.

The next day, I said to Jim, I wonder if someone has taken him yet, and that maybe we rushed into giving him away. Jim also said he felt bad and asked me if I wanted him to go pick Barney up. It didn't take me but a second to say yes. Jim said "but if we do get him back he will have to go to dog obedience class", which we agreed on.

Well when Jim arrived at the SPCA to pick up Barney, the same caretaker was there and said he was expecting Jim to come back to get him. He said I just knew you would be back.

Jim's New Work Partner

Well now that Barney was going to officially be part of our family, there were going to be ground rules put down.

- He was going to be walked everyday,
- He was going to go to obedience school
- He was going to go to work with Jim

Jim was an appliance repairman (Maytag) at that time of his life. So he had his own van and would go directly to his service calls from home. So it was convenient to take Barney along with him, that way he would be taken care of and he wouldn't be lonely. (Not Jim . . . . the dog). This was the start of a real close and tight relationship between Barney and Jim. Barney was Jim's dog.

I felt very comfortable at work knowing that Barney was with Jim, and knowing that the house would look the same as we left it in the morning,
(no chewing on the floor moldings' or legs of the chairs, or scratched doors, or snagging the carpet with his nails and then pulling on the snag until it was a couple of feet long) was very comforting, and Jim had himself a work partner. Even at times when Jim went through a drive-thru for lunch, he would purchase a cheeseburger for Barney, and the employee at the window thought it was so cute that Barney was getting his own order.

He ended up being a pretty special and spoiled dog.

The only problem with him being with Jim all day is when at home he really didn't listen to me much; he took his commands from Jim. Mind you I fed him and bathed him, dried him, combed him brought him home his treats and spoiled him with gifts and spent time with him, but he was still very loyal to Jim and nothing could change that, I was second best. Even when Jim and I played around, Barney would growl and get between us. He always looked at me when he growled. I knew he would never hurt me, he just didn't want me hurting Jim, it was that, or he thought Jim belonged to him. I really didn't know, but when you looked into his eyes you could see that he didn't like not being involved in whatever was going on.

Barney liked people but only if he knew them, he did not like strangers. It was embarrassing when we took him camping with us and while sitting in the car if a cyclist rode by he would go crazy and bark at them. He loved to sit between Jim and myself all the time, even in the family van mainly because he was so jealous if he wasn't the center of attention.

When winter came and the roads were really bad for driving, Jim would take me to work, as I was about to get into the van, Barney had jumped onto the front seat before I sat down. I said "hey, wait a minute you're the dog", I don't care if you sit here everyday I am not sitting in the back of a cargo van! He got down with a push on his rear end from me. He would sit between the two front seats and he wouldn't budge.

Barney loved winter, playing in the snow

Oh he was something else. We had a nickname for him; we would call him Mr. Barnes. Mainly because he always thought he was the boss. He would also always have the last word. If I got mad at him for something, he would grunt at me, if I said something after that he would grunt again. He had a real attitude that dog.

Barney was such a special dog, he knew when you were in pain or upset. He would spend time with you when you were lying on the couch or in bed sick. He would be at your side. He would kiss you, and every time you moved he would look up at you. He would rest his head on your hip, or legs, he was very sensitive, he picked up on all vibes. He was just the best. Something about his eyes, they were like human eyes; you could really see his soul through his eyes. They were a beautiful brown color, and just by looking at his eyes you could see so much character in him. We would be sitting on the couch doing whatever, and he would come up to one of us and just rest his chin on our knee, and his eyes would just stare straight through you. It was like he was telling us, I'm here too you know and I don't want to be ignored, pay attention to me. Sometimes he would just nudge our hand to the top of his head to be petted, or even grunt at us, whatever he could do to get attention. Seriously, sometimes he was worse than a child. He wanted attention 24/7.

Doctor Barnes taking care of the patient

More than just a dog

It was sometime in October and I found out I was pregnant, the babies due date was for July, so it gave us plenty of time to get Barney trained. Jim enrolled him into dog obedience school. The course was every Saturday for about 6 weeks; he decided to be the one to take him since he was really his dog. This was fine with me. I don't really know how much Barney got out of these classes. One good piece of information we got out of it was the trainer told us that we had a Portuguese Water Dog. We had no idea what that was, she knew her dogs, and told us to go get a book on pure bred dogs. He had all the markings, even the vet said that he was exactly what she said.

We got to thinking; it was around the time that the pups were born we read in the local paper that someone had stolen a pregnant Portuguese Water Dog. Was his mother the stolen dog? Wow if that was the case then we got a pure bred for $25.00. They sold between $1500.-1800.00 depending on where you purchased them. (14 years later when we bought our second Portuguese Water dog at the price of $1200. but because he was already 3 months old we got him for $800, we found him through the internet). We also found out more about their personality.

Yes, the new information we found out made so much sense. It matched their PWD's personality.

Anyways, back to his dog obedience classes. What a joke! Jim would tell me the stories of things that Barney would do, I only went to the class once, because the instructor told the owners that only one person should be there as to not distract the dog. This was probably about the 3rd week in;

we just wanted to see for ourselves how he was making out. Mainly, Barney did his own thing, didn't like to be told what to do. The one day that my son and I went to the class, we were sitting in the bleachers, and Barney saw us . . . . oops. When the trainer called for Barney to come to her he came to us instead wagging his tail. We yelled back at him stop, go back. How embarrassing, the other dogs just sat still.

At the end of the course, Jim would come home with Barney and a red ribbon he said Barney came in 5th in his obedience class. I said oh well that's not so bad at least he didn't come in last. To that Jim replied, 5th was last place. . . . . Oh.

A Brief History and Profile of the Breed

Once we knew what type of dog we actually had, we did some research, and it all made sense, his energy, his huge personality, stubbornness, attitude, constant hole digger, his want for companionship all the time. He was very jealous of Jim and myself, did not like it when we hugged or kissed or just plain didn't pay attention to him.

This breed's origin is in Portugal the weight can range or should range between 42-60 lbs for males and 35-50 lbs for females. Our Barney was 42 lbs. Now our 2nd water dog Theodore he was 65 lbs at full grown and then later tipped the scales at one time at 103 lbs.

www.canadasguidetodogs.com/ortugesewater.htm

The Portuguese water dog known as the Cao de Agua "dog of the water" and the Portuguese Fishing Dog, was once popular all along Portugal's coast where he was said to be prized by fishermen as a companion and guard dog. During this time, the dogs lived and worked on boats where they herded fish into nets, retrieved lost tackle or broken nets and acted as couriers from boat to boat to shore. These tasks required that the dogs be excellent swimmers. They were also capable of diving underwater to retrieve gear and to prevent fish from escaping from the nets. Modern technology, however, nearly caused the extinction of the breed.

Although there are many theories about the Water dog's history, there is no doubt that he has an ancient ancestry and is said to predate the

Poodle, in pre-Christian times, it is said that the "water dog" was seen as nearly sacred. The breed was first brought to the United States in the late 1960s and by early 1970, there were only 25 known Portuguese Water Dogs in the world. However, because of dedicated breeders, by 1981 there were over 500 dogs in the U.S. today, there are thousands living all over the world and though still not a common breed, it is no longer rare or in danger of extinction.

The Porty (Portuguese Water Dog) is exceptionally intelligent, has an endless amount of stamina, is brave, and spirited. He is also a devoted and loyal companion and an alert guard dog. This is not, however, the dog for everyone. Make note incase after reading this book you want to go out and purchase one.

His high activity level makes him an excellent working dog and companion but he needs daily exercise and requires direction, so if you are living in an apartment or condo, or have a very small yard, this would not be the dog for you.

He is people-oriented and does not do well in a kennel environment or left alone for long periods of time. We know this first hand the first time we left Barney in a kennel for 4 days he was around 1 year old, when we arrived back to pick him up we were told he never ate the whole time we were gone and just sat in a corner and wouldn't budge, he would not allow the caretaker to enter his kennel to take him for a walk, he growl and showed his teeth if he came anywhere near him. So after that episode the kennel owner told us he would not take him back. We did find another kennel a couple of years later that we would drop him off periodically, but more than not we took him with us, camping, etc.

The Portuguese Water Dog thrives on being part of a family and generally gets along well with children and other pets. Though not aggressive, he is alert and protective making him a good watchdog of home and property.

Today the Portuguese Water Dog is seen participating in various dog sports and activities, including show ring, obedience, water dog trials through the Portuguese Water Dog Club of America and agility. He is also seen working as a Therapy Dog and Assistance Dog.

We were also told that they are used in San Francisco at the baseball stadium, when the balls go over the wall they send out the dogs to retrieve the balls from the ocean. Quite a versatile dog.

The average life expectancy for the Portuguese Water Dog is 12-15 years. They generally mature slowly and remain active well into their senior years. We can verify that both our Porty's matured around 7 years of age.

Like all breeds of dogs, the Portuguese Water Dog may be susceptible to certain genetic disorders. The greatest of concerns with this breed are as follows:

Hip dysplasia, Progressive Retinal Atrophy, Storage Disease, Juvenile Dilated Cardiomyopathy, Follicular Dysplasia and Addison's disease . . . . Of which Theodore's mother and sister passed away within 8 months of each other.

So if you are thinking of purchasing a Porty it is very important to be selective in choosing a responsible and reputable breeder. Ensure that the prospective puppy's parents have all health clearances. Breeding of any dog should not be done until after they have been proven to be free of evidence of significant hereditary diseases, including those listed above.

The Porty is a medium-sized, strong and robust dog with a penetrating, almost piercing glaze in his eyes.

Look into my eyes

He is said to have excellent eye sight and a fair nose. Ours had more than a fair nose; Barney would sniff anyone and everyone's crotch. Theodore on the other hand would sniff anyone and everyone's rear end, even us everyday, every chance he got, so you had to watch bending around him.

He is a very good swimmer and has webbed feet. He has non-shedding coat that may be either wavy or curly, with no undercoat. Because of his non-shedding coat, the breed may be a good choice for allergy sufferers. The coat is thick and profuse and covers the whole body evenly. He is either black, white, or various shades of brown. He may also be combinations of black or brown with white. The Porty has an effortless and balanced trotting gait, displaying a proud carriage and a contented attitude.

He carries his tail high in a ring over the back. His walking gait is light with short steps and his gallop is very energetic.

The Water Dog is the only breed that can jump from the water into a boat without help. It has been common in Portugal since the 12th Century.

Mind you not all dogs are the same, we always had to help ours back into the boat, could be the shape and style of the boat, that I am not sure. Throwing toys out into the water and having them retrieve it is something our Porty's loved to do. Our Theodore even jumped off the boat and swam under the hull and out the other side. We would have the ladder extended from the back of the boat and when he tired he would hang his paws on the steps of the ladder until he was ready to swim again.

Barney Loving his boat rides. . . . can never get enough of that open air.

I Don't Like His "I Think I'm King Behavior"

Barney was not always a well behaved dog; he would run away every chance he got. In the summer he would take off to any of the neighbors' that had a sprinkler on. He would just stand there with the sprinkler soaking him and trying to bite the water. One of the neighbors was watering his lawn with just a hose and Barney would run onto his lawn, the neighbor would spray Barney to get rid of him, but little did he know that that was just luring him in. I would just look out the window and laugh, until I knew the neighbor got fed up, then I would go over and get him because it was useless calling him, he just chose to ignore me. We had a creek in our backyard it was only about 4-6 inches deep in the summer and Barney would lay in the creek to cool off, from a distance he looked like an alligator with his legs sprawled out behind him, and only the top of his head and back to be seen, chin and all in the water.

Barney for some strange reason didn't like other dogs; maybe he thought they were beneath him. I don't know. Or maybe he thought they would get some of our attention. If someone came to the door and rang the doorbell . . . . Oh God the barking, he just hated anyone coming to the door. We would have to hang on to his collar to open the door . . . that's if we couldn't force him into a room and close the door, but once the person came in, i.e. someone he knew, then they were his best friend and he wouldn't let them go, he wanted them to pet, pet and pet some more.

One day I noticed a women walking up our driveway, so I quickly opened the door to tell her not to bother coming all the way up because of the dog, but Barney was too fast for me, she was coming door to door selling something, I didn't get a chance to find out what, anyways Barney ran out at her barking, of course scared her and jumped up and ripped her nylons. Oh I was mad at him. He never hurt her, just scared her. I could never figure out what his problem was.

The same went when he looked out the window and saw someone walking, especially running or riding a bike, he would bark so furiously, we could never understand why. Even when he was in the car he would bark at people going past us. The vet told us to try different things which we did. Once we used the spiked collar, but I brought that back, I thought it was just inhumane. Then we tried the collar with a plastic container that sprays his nose with a bitter taste every time he barks that worked for a while until he got used to the flavor. That was a waste of money. I tried using a spray bottle on him with water that sometimes worked, we tried a rolled up newspaper, ya right, and he would grab it and try to tear it apart. So whenever we were expecting people to come over we would keep an eye outside and open the door before they rang the bell, or just lock Barney in a room until they came into the house.

Sometimes he would get loose out of the house or yard, and we hoped that we found him before someone came down the street because he would run after them and bark, he never hurt anyone just wanted to show them who ran the neighborhood. When he was a young pup, he got out just when the mail lady came; he wouldn't get out of her way and kept biting at her shoe so she kicked him. We called the post office and complained about her, she had told them that he attacked her. We were furious, how could anyone kick a little puppy, he wasn't more than 4 months old at that time.

*This was him a small fur ball,
couldn't hurt more than a bug*

We think that was the start of his dislike of people coming to his door, whenever the mail got put through our mail slot which dropped on the front entrance floor, Barney would attack the mail and rip it, until we set up a box for it to drop into. He also didn't like people in uniforms, which explained lots because the mail lady that kicked him had worn an official government post office uniform. She actually tainted him for the rest of his life by kicking him.

My First Birthday Party

December 7 was my son's birthday, which was Barney's first birthday party; Barney was now 1 year old. He loved being around a lot of people, the more people the more attention and petting, so we decided to dress him up a bit and he really didn't mind. The kids thought it was funny, it went over well, the only other time we dressed him up was in the winter with a coat. That was the beginning of something different, in time, when we got our other dogs I would dress them up just because it looked so cute.

My First Christmas Alone

Well it was Barney's first Christmas alone, on Christmas Eve we left him at home and went to my parents, we always celebrated on Christmas Eve. (my family being European) and then the next day in the late morning or early afternoon we would spend Christmas day with my husbands family). We didn't dare ask to bring Barney along. Christmas Eve we were gone for maybe 3-4 hours, so it really didn't give Barney much time to do too much wrong, he was actually a good boy. So on Christmas morning, we had our own little family celebration, Barney got treats and toys, we played with Justin and his new toys and Barney, we had a great morning. It was time to go to Jim's parents around 2:00 and we knew we would be gone for several hours because we were having Christmas dinner at his parents. So I didn't want to feed Barney too early, so I just left his food in his dish and plenty of water, his toys were left out for him to play with and a raw hide bone for chewing, since he was still really a puppy he did lots of chewing and we were hoping that he would concentrate on his bone, not anything else.

We arrived home around 8:00pm, when we drove up the driveway we were relieved that the house was still standing, the front door was still intact. Now we just prayed that the inside was as we left it. We opened the front door and saw the tip of the Christmas tree on the floor. OH NO!!! Barney knocked the tree over, he had been chewing on the Christmas lights, Thank God we didn't leave it plugged in, I guess he pulled on the light cord as he chewed and knocked the tree over, that gave him many other items to chew on. When he knocked the tree over it also knocked over our television, the fall of the television thankfully just cracked the frame, the screen was still in one piece, but the tree also knocked over our anniversary clock that was sitting on the fireplace mantle. We were so freaked out; we didn't know where to start the cleanup. I also had some candles on the coffee table that he ate. When I checked out the rest of the house everything else seemed to be fine except the kitchen. On the counter I had a platter of chocolates, the platter was pushed to the back of the counter, so I have no idea how he could have gotten to it. The platter was pulled forward and all the chocolate was gone. My God, dogs can die from eating chocolate, it speeds up their heart rate, but not Barney he had a cast iron stomach. We immediately let him outside to do his business; by the time he was done he had a very colorful poop in the front yard; I guess the candles had gone through his system after all those hours.

I just wanted to relax when we got home and have a drink, but Barney made sure that we were going to pay for leaving him alone on Christmas Day. That was the last time we left him alone for Christmas, from then on we took him to our families until he grew up.

Another member to our family

Well almost a year went by and I gave birth to another boy. We weren't sure how Barney would react to a baby. Our first son was already 5 when we got Barney, so a newborn would be a new toy to Barney.

Faithful Barney always there

He actually did exceptionally well, he licked him a lot, and sniffed him a lot, and he even guarded him, Aaron was born in July, so I had him out on the deck in his stroller a lot, and Barney would lay on the deck beside the stroller, and when Aaron would stir or make a sound, Barney would jump up and look into the stroller. While I was at home on maternity leave, Jim left Barney with me. He felt it would be a good time for Barney to get to know the rest of us better and then it also gave Jim some alone time too. Although many times Jim would come home for his lunch break and have a short nap with Barney.

Barney was a real family dog. I think he thought he was a human, when we watched tv in the family room, he would sit on the ottoman with his rear on the cushion, and his front legs on the floor. He loved being around us, actually he was his worst when left alone even if only for a little while. When we went out and came back you could see that he had been nervous while at home, his eyes would have a bulging look to them and he would be panting by the time we got back. Theodore our future dog did the exact same thing. The Porty's always want company, Barney was one spoiled dog, and we loved him so much he was like another child. I would bring him a treat home every time I went grocery shopping, it got to the point when I brought in the groceries and left the bags on the floor, he would snoop through the bags and grab what was his. One Christmas I had brought home a rawhide candy cane that I wanted to put away in his stocking, I forgot that he was going to snoop in the bag, I had left the kitchen for a few moments and by the time I came back he was in the dining room chewing on it. I was mad but at the same time laughed, he was very smart.

He was getting pretty big, but that didn't matter we carried him around from time to time, just to spoil him, he slept on the bed most nights, he would like to cuddle with us. Sometimes he just got in the way though.

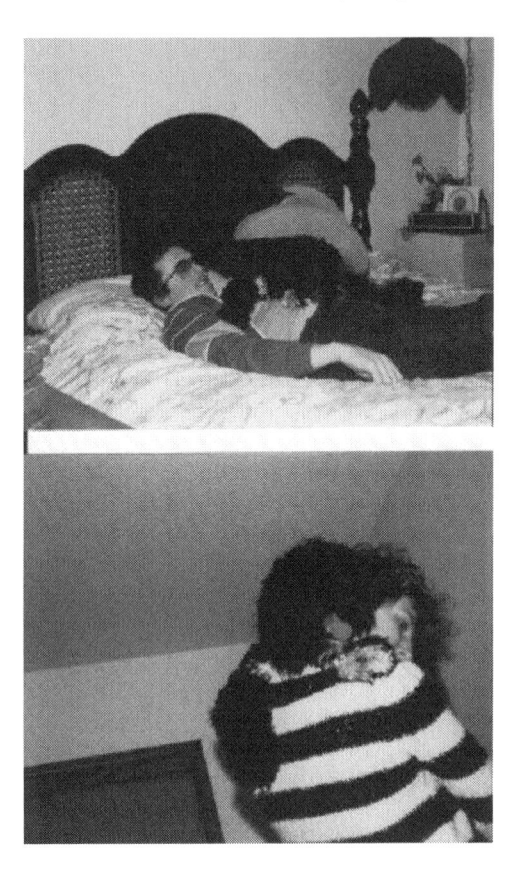

But he loved being pampered, I believe that he thought he was part human, even when Jim played piano, Barney would lay on the floor beside him or even on the piano bench and he would actually howl while Jim played music, it was hilarious, I had never heard anything like it before.

Barney loved music

If you tried to take him off the bench while Jim was playing the piano, he would growl at you, his place was beside Jim and he would not leave until Jim did, or if you had some food to offer him.

Holidays With Or Without Him

Well we had a weekend banquet that we had to go to at Qualicum Beach on Vancouver Island, we had family taking care of the kids, and we didn't know what we would do with Barney because we didn't want to leave him in a Kennel again, not until he was a bit older. So we spoke to a neighbor boy that knew Barney very well, and he agreed to come over everyday and feed him and take him for walks. We gated the top of the steps up to the living room from the basement so that Barney had the whole run of the basement and could come up the stairs to the living room but not enter it. Jim's dad would also come over to visit Barney; now remember we were going to be gone only 3 days. We had moved our master bedroom to the basement sometime ago, so Barney should be comfortable down there having full run of the recreation room and bedroom. There were also french doors in the rec room going out to the backyard so he had plenty of light coming in and could see outside.

When we came home Barney was so excited to see us. The neighbor boy said that he was fine, he would come to the basement door and take Barney out 3 times a day and also feed him, and he said that he wasn't a problem at all. Although . . . . Al, Jim's dad said it was a totally different story with him. He came over once and brought him a weiner, he came through the front door, he called Barney several times at the top of the stairs, and he got no answer. So he decided to go downstairs to check on him, he was worried that something could be wrong. He walked through the rec room, and still no Barney, so then he entered into the bedroom and called him again, all of a sudden he heard a growl and saw Barney, his lips were curled showing Al his teeth, even though he knew Al very well he still didn't want anything to do with him. He actually chased Al up the stairs, he scared the daylight out of him, Al said he threw pieces of the weiner to Barney but he didn't want it. You see when Jim's parents would come visit us, Al would always bring Barney a weiner as a treat, that was a good way to get the dog to be his friend, but it didn't work this time. He said that Barney had come half way up the stairs when he chased him. So Al left pieces of the weiner on the steps but Barney didn't want it. He said that was the only time he came to visit him. That told us of how freaked Barney got when we weren't home. Although like I said earlier the neighbor boy said he was fine, was he or was he just lying for Barney.

He didn't use the inside of the house to do his business at all so he must have gotten outside for his walks. He also didn't destroy anything in the house which made us happy. When we did get home the weiner was gone so he must have eaten it when Al left. We were shocked when he told us what Barney did, its not like Al was a stranger.

Later on when we moved to the Okanagan Valley 4 ½ hours to the interior of British Columbia, we would purchase a 5th wheel trailer and take Barney camping with us. Oh how he loved it, we had it put on a permanent spot in Penticton on Skaha Lake, this way we could keep our boat moored on the lake and spend weekends during the summer at the trailer, it was like our summer cabin.

Barney knew when we loaded the vehicle for the weekend where we were going; you could see the excitement in his body. (By this time we had our 3rd and final son, so when we packed the vehicle, it was full. Not just with supplies and luggage but with bodies Barney's included). He would get to go swimming a lot, and spend the evenings with us at the fire pit and eat wieners'. He was always in the camping spirit when we went to Penticton. I think one of the reasons why he enjoyed it so much is because we mainly lived outside on the deck or on the boat. We would ride our bikes down the KVR (Kettle Valley Rail) trail and he would follow. We'd make several stops for him to go jump in the lake and then we would find a nice private outcrop of rocks and just sit and vegetate, he really liked that. He also liked our trips because he would get a treat "pepperoni" he loved that stuff, we'd give him a small piece every now and then for that special treat. In the evenings after the kids were bunked down Jim and I would light the torches on the deck and play soft music and have a few drinks, we would lay on our lawn beds and Barney would have his pillow and lay between us on the floor. When I was ready to go to bed I went myself, Jim would like to stay out on the deck until maybe 2:00am in the morning and Barney wouldn't come in until Jim did.

Now even though the bed in the 5th wheel was a queen size bed, it wasn't as large as a normal queen, but that didn't matter to Barney, he refused to lay on the floor or on the couch. It had to always be on the bed between our feet.

Playing cowboy with dad—4 days before his passing

Drying up from his swim . . . Life is good

Even when the kids set up the tent in the backyard Barney would camp with them . . . . Just until bedtime then he wanted to sleep on the bed with us. We were never lucky enough to have a night to ourselves on the bed.

Visits From Oma

My mom, (Oma as the kids called her because of her Austrian heritage) just loved Barney, he really was the first pet into our family, he adored her, and she would bring him treats all the time. Actually, when she comes to visit from the Coast she over feeds him. I would tell her "No" he is going to get fat, she'd say "oh but I'm only giving him a little bit", the next time I would turn around and her hand is coming up from under the table again and she would laugh. Oh she meant well, she spoiled him like the rest of us, but Barney knew how to push people's buttons he always got what he wanted.

I'll never forget one of her visits, we were renting a house in Vernon the Okanagan Valley while our house was being built, and this was her first visit to our place since we moved here from the coast. She flew in and I picked her up from the airport in Kelowna. Well of course she got the best greeting anyone could get from Barney and he didn't give her a chance to even get in the house all the way, so she just dropped everything in the entrance way of the front door so she could play with him. Then we headed up the stairs and I told her I would go down and bring her luggage up to her bedroom for her, so she left her luggage and purse in the entrance way. The living room, front entrance and stairway were an open concept. It was only about 6 steps to get to the living room so you could see anything going on at the front door. Well as I walked towards the stairs to get her belongings I saw Barney peeing in her purse. I was in shock I didn't know if I should yell at him . . . because if I did then she would know what he did and their was no way I could get it cleaned up before she noticed. If I didn't get mad at him he would think it was alright, and I still wouldn't get it cleaned out before she noticed. Also, how could I explain to her if she caught me with her purse, dumping everything out and actually going through her purse? Remember this was all going through my mind in a matter of about 2 seconds. So I just let it out! Even while I was yelling at him he continued to pee in her purse. Everything that sat in the middle of her purse got wet; you see she had her purse open all the way. She was not very happy with Barney, but that didn't last to long. I still can't figure out to this day why he did it. Maybe, marking his territory on her purse?

Barney was a comedian; some of the things he did made you laugh so hard. While she was visiting, Jim lay on the floor and played with the kids, while he did that, my mom and I sat on the couch and watched Barney carefully go over to Jim and pull his wallet out of his rear pant pocket. Jim didn't even notice, Barney was so careful not to disturb him and pulled it out ever so gently. My mom and I just laughed and laughed, we had to tell Jim what happened because he never would have noticed. On one other day, he pulled my mom's wallet out of her purse, without anyone knowing. I was accused of teaching him to pick pocket for me. Of course I did not.

Barney at 12 years with Oma

*Approx 10 weeks before Barney's passing . . . . .
Oma spoiled Barney like he was her grandchild*

When Oma would come to visit, she would steal my Barney, she would try to get him to stay in her room at night . . . . She said he kept her warm. He'd go with her and plop himself on her bed, until we went to bed, nothing would keep him from our bed.

Barney was everyone's best friend

Barney's Last Chapter

One day we were checking Barnes for ticks, it's a normal thing to do during the spring and fall when you live in the Okanagan Valley. Anyways we noticed a lump around his shoulder area on his front leg, at first we thought that it was just fatty tissue, so we kept an eye on it and within a month noticed that it got larger and he seemed to be limping, we brought him to the vet that we normally took him too. They took x-rays and told us that he had a tumor and that it should be removed it was cancerous (osteocercoma) as it was called. So we had it removed but there was no guarantee that it wouldn't come back, within a few months he seemed to have trouble again in that area, so we brought him back and they took more x-rays and said that the bone was so fragile and there were so many holes in the bone from the cancer eating away at it and that they felt the best thing to do was to remove his front leg. Oh My God . . . . NO WAY!!! Barney was 12 years old, there was no way we would do something like that to him now, how cruel is that to go into surgery with 4 legs and come out with 3, you can't explain to a dog why you did that to him, maybe if he was still a young dog, but not at his age. So we decided to go to another vet and got the same response, remove his leg. We talked so much about this and said there has to be another way to help him without destroying what he has left of his life.

Well my husband found a way, like usual he always finds an answer to our problems . . . . And the answer to our problem; he was Dr. E Kaplan a special doctor that would end up giving Barney another 2 years to live. A precious 2 years that we would cherish with him. Jim phoned the College of Veterinarians in Saskatchewan, he told them our dilemma and they gave us a phone number for a vet in Lake Country (Kelowna area) Dr. E. Kaplan; he was our hero.

Dr. Kaplan is the only veterinarian in the area (at that time anyways, things may have changed now) that specialized in cancer within animals. He obviously had a lot of knowledge and training because he truly helped us. After taking x-rays he said thank goodness you didn't have his leg removed because we can help him in other ways. He told us to give him a number of things, i.e. shark cartilage pills, glucosamine . . . and of course pain medication, along with pills that had a special chemo in it; also he had a special food recipe for him with a lot of herbs and natural foods for him.

Our last weekend with Barney

It was the Labour Day weekend in September we decided to spend the last long weekend of the summer with the kids and Barney at Penticton in our 5th wheel again. Barney was very lethargic that weekend, all he wanted to do was lay on the deck. At this point he couldn't walk much at all, but this weekend seemed to be much worse, we actually had to carry him off the deck to the lawn so he could go to the bathroom. We were really worried as to where this was leading. We knew that the inevitable was coming, he had gone into remission twice now and not likely a third time, he was 14 now and that was the lifespan of this breed, so you see even though Barney was diagnosed with cancer at the age of 12 he still lived his full life span thanks to Dr. Kaplan.

*Preferring to lie on the grass with not much energy
And not very hungry anymore*

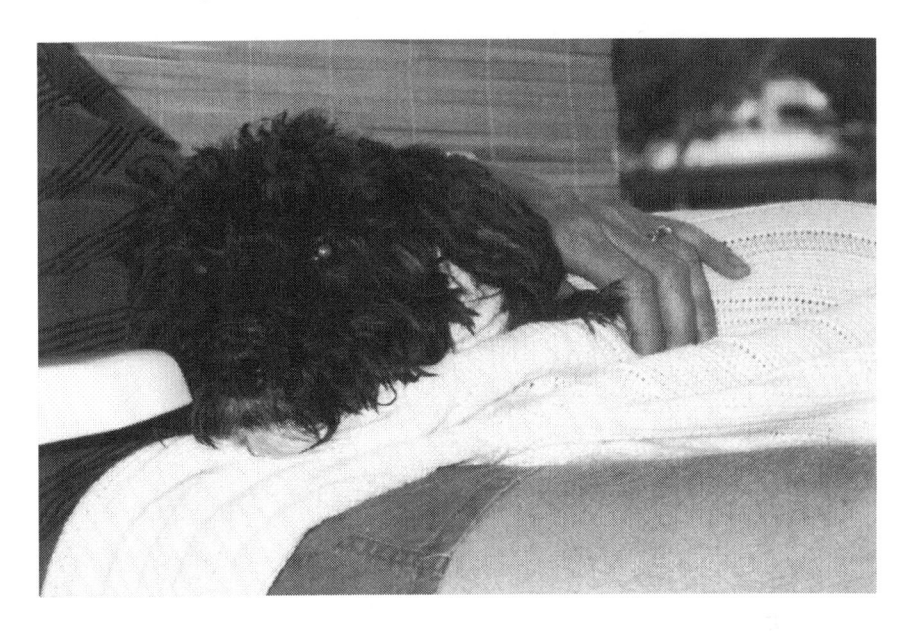

Not feeling too well

Anyways, the neighbor next door had a yellow lab, very gentle dog, he would come over and sniff Barney while laying on the deck, he knew there was something wrong. I would put a blanket on the deck for him and then cover him up. He would just lay there and watch us, we felt so bad for him, and we loved him so much that it just tore us apart to see him like this, so lifeless. That evening Jim carried him to our bed and at sometime in the early hours of the morning Barney had gotten up probably to turn himself around and I heard a loud crack and then he yelped and cried, I jumped up I knew he broke a bone in his leg. Oh my God! Poor Barney, we called the answering service at the vet, it was now Saturday morning and they told us to bring him in, we knew this was the end. It would take us about 1 ½ hours to drive to Lake Country from Penticton. We woke up the kids and told them what had happened and where we were going. Everyone was sad and had trouble keeping the tears back. We tried to make him as comfortable as we possibly could. The past month we have been giving Barney his favorite foods because we knew the end was near, if he gained weight . . . who cared it wasn't going to kill him the cancer was. Anyways one of his favorites' was McDonald's cheeseburgers, my mom had come to visit the month prior and whenever we came back from town she would get me to stop at McDonald's to buy him a cheeseburger. His other favorite was pepperoni, man he loved that stuff, so on his last drive to the vet, Jim made a stop on the way to pick up some pepperoni for Barney. It was so hard on us knowing that this was his last bit of food he would ever eat, he had to of known too because it didn't interest him at all.

Barney sat between Aaron and Daniel on the trip to the vet, they hugged him while he laid his head on Aaron's lap, and they tried to tempt him with pepperoni, but he was just not interested.

We arrived at the veterinarians' office, no one wanting to get out; the weight that seemed to pull my heart down into my stomach was so heavy, and it was the same for the rest of the family. It would have been so easy for me to just start bawling but I couldn't do that because of the kids, I had to keep swallowing hard to keep the tears back. Jim said lets not bring him inside with everyone else. Let's sit outside on the lawn with him where we have some privacy and where it will be quiet. So we laid him on the ground and sat around him while Jim let Dr. Kaplan know where we were. He had come out to check on him and just reassured us that there was nothing else that he could do for Barney and for his sake this would be the best thing we could ever do for him, to take away his pain and let him go to his final resting place. So what Dr. Kaplan did first was give him a shot to relax him so that he was in no pain at all, but still coherent and we could spend time with him and say our goodbyes, we probably sat outside with Barney for about 45 minutes and reminisced of all the good times we had with him and of all the times he made us so mad and I even brought up the time as a pup when we brought him to the pound because we couldn't take it anymore, the two kids weren't even born then, we laughed and we cried, we each took a turn and looked into his eyes and told him something special. Except for Aaron he didn't want to say anything. In reality, he probably had a lot he wanted to say but couldn't speak for fear of breaking down and crying. I sat there on the grass with Barney's head on my lap and looked into his eyes and told him when he goes to heaven Opa will be waiting for him and that when its my turn to go that he was to meet me in Heaven.

Dr. Kaplan came back with two needles, one would be to make him go to sleep and the other was to stop his heart. He asked us if we were ready, we said one more goodbye to Barney and I could see in his eyes he knew we were hurting too, I could feel that he knew what was happening and it was like he was telling us through his eyes that it was okay to let him go and that he needed to be rid of his pain. I knew he loved us and through his eyes I also knew that he was thanking us for giving him such a happy and fun life. So we gave the doctor the okay, he administered the second shot, and we watched as Barney slowly closed his eyes and we continuously told him that we loved him. Then the tears started to pour from all of us. Dr. Kaplan was so gentle and his voice so kind, he knew how much we loved Barney as if he was our child. Daniel asked if he could have some of Barney's tail hair, so Dr. Kaplan left us to get some scissors and a blanket, he asked Daniel what part of the hair he wanted and then cut it and put it into a baggie and gave it to Daniel. Then he administered the last shot, within about 3 seconds Barney's heart stopped . . . and then it was over, our dear best friend was gone, it felt like our child had died. Dr. Kaplan used his stethoscope to make sure that the heart had stopped, he again told us how sorry he was and we kissed Barney one more time, and then he wrapped him in a blanket and carried him into the building. That was so difficult watching him carry him away, his limp body, never to see him again . . . . At least not in this lifetime. We ended up having Barney cremated and put some of his ashes under the cherry tree in the backyard, his favorite shady place to lay in the summertime. Some more was placed at our favorite campsite where he loved to swim at the lake. The rest I still have to this date, my husband and I had agreed which ever one of us dies first will take Barney with them.

BARNEY
SEPTEMBER 1985-SEPTEMBER 6, 1999
RIP

The drive back to Penticton was very somber, I had rather continued on home, but for the kids sake we went back to Penticton. The neighbors' had all known what had happened and were very kind with their condolences and cards, they had all liked Barney. I just couldn't stop crying; I called my mom on the cell and told her that Barney was gone. She started crying on the phone.

On the Monday when we came home it was so hard going into the house without him and seeing his bed, bowls and toys laying around. My sister-in-law sent me this poem after Barney had passed away. It made me feel a lot more at ease and lifted some of the pain from my heart.

Rainbow Bridge

Just this side of heaven is a place called Rainbow Bridge.
When an animal dies, that has been especially close to someone here,
that pet goes to Rainbow Bridge.

There are meadows and hills for all of our special friends so they can run
and play together. There is plenty of food, water and sunshine, and our friends
are warm and comfortable.

All the animals who had been ill and old are restored to health and vigor; those
who were hurt or maimed are made whole and strong again, just as we remember
them in our dreams of days and times gone by.

The animals are happy and content, except for one small thing; they each miss
someone very special to them, who had to be left behind.

They all run and play together, but the day comes when one suddenly stops and
looks into the distance. His bright eyes are intent; his eager body quivers. Suddenly,
he begins to run from the group, flying over the green grass, his legs carrying him
faster and faster.

You have been spotted and when you and your special friend finally meet, you cling
together in joyous reunion, never to be parted again. The happy kisses rain upon your
face; your hands again caress the beloved head, and you look once more into the trusting
eyes of your pet, so long gone from your life but never absent from your heart.

Author Unknown . . .

to the memorials

Life after Barney

Two weeks went by and I could not stand being without him, I still kept crying, everyone was still sad and missed him terribly, but I couldn't stop the tears from coming. So what we did was the start of something that could not be stopped, I needed another dog, not a replacement of Barney but just another Portuguese Water Dog, I needed that unconditional love that the dog brings, our family needed it. Which then turned into 4 dogs, we thought our lives had changed with Barney that was a cake walk.

Our 2ⁿᵈ Generation Kids

Well Jim finally found us another Porty, he found him on the internet through breeders. Our new dog was in Alberta, he was one of two left of a litter of 7, there was one girl and one boy left, and they were already 3 months old, so we got a better deal. We had to go through interviews just to make the breeder feel that we were capable and responsible in taking care of him. We told her that we had one for 14 years. She said well if you have already had one then you know what you will be getting into and I am sure you will be a good owner, (this was after several more questions). So I went to the bank and did an electronic payment to her. We were to meet her friend 1 week later in Penticton at the dog show to pick up our new dog. Our new puppy was coming from Canmore Alberta and to Penticton it is about an 8-9 hour drive. The woman that brought our new dog said that he was a good boy except for the constant chewing on her stick shift. He hid behind her like a little child, Jim and I both bent down and put our hand out to him to coax him over, but he was very shy and got to know the woman during the long drive to Penticton, so he trusted her, now we were strangers.

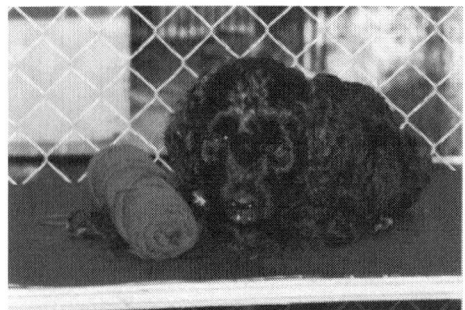

8 weeks old. Pictures from his breeder

Folly (mom)—Alberta
Won for best in Breed

Dad—from New York

We were camping in Penticton with our kids on this weekend in September, it was already dusk when we met and picked up our new dog. By the time we got back to the campsite it was getting darker. We took our new puppy for a walk and he seemed to be nervous, we thought it was because he was now amongst strangers, but what we didn't realize right away was he was actually afraid of his own shadow which was created while we walked with the moon shining behind us. It was hilarious, he would see his shadow ahead of him and stare at it, he would stop and be afraid to go forward and sometimes jump away from it but the strangest thing . . . . It kept following him.

We hadn't named him yet; we were throwing names around but couldn't come up with anything definite. When it was bedtime we put him on the floor with blankets, but to no avail he kept whining and drove us crazy, so I let him sleep on the bed. Wrong thing to do because for all the nights afterwards he thought that was his permanent spot to sleep.

That morning, we decided on a name for him, because he looked like a teddy bear with all that hair, we called him Theodore . . . . Theo for short.

It was another beautiful sunny warm morning, we thought what better time to take him for a swim, I figured, he is a water dog he should start getting used to the water. We walked on the dock and tried to get him to go into the water, but he wasn't in agreement with us, so we just pushed him in, he was not too pleased with what just happened.

He was a hilarious dog, we were camping for 2 nights, and we learnt a lot about him in that short time. He already had a personality and a temper, he would fight for what he wanted and loved to play, and chewing was his pass time. He has such an adorable face, we walked him throughout the campsite and met several people throughout our walk, and they all wanted to see Theo but he would shy away from them and hide behind us. It was so cute, and now he barks at people walking along the street because he thinks he owns the streets. Oh he has himself quite the personality, my sister came for a visit once while we were camping, and she brought her cat and kept the cat in her pet carrier kennel. She placed the kennel on the deck and of course Theo had to stick his nose where it didn't belong and sniffed at what was in the cage. Well the cat hissed at him and he went running off the deck like a bolt of lightening and tried to hide under the deck. What a big baby, afraid of a cat, yet if he is confronted with another dog he will bark at him and try to show that he was the boss.

He became very comfortable with us in a very short time. Remember this was the first weekend that he was with us. That evening it started to cool down really fast (it was early October) Summer was over and Fall was fast approaching. I sat at the dinette set in the recreation vehicle and read a book, before I knew it Theo was sitting beside me, being nosy, oh he couldn't sit across from me he had to be right tight and snug beside me.

Strange Dog

The next morning at breakfast he decided again that the kitchen nook was where he was supposed to sit.

We had ourselves one crazy dog, I don't know who taught him to sit like this but it wasn't going to be something we would let him continue. It was funny though, I swear he was more human than dog.

Theo took our minds off of the sadness of Barney's passing, we would never forget Barney, but the pain was getting lesser and lesser. The two dogs may have been of the same breed, but they were two different identities, even though they did have many of the same traits.

The last evening before going home we had ourselves a nice dinner that consisted of smokies over the fire. One of our neighbors' took our picture with the newest member of the family. That was a first family portrait with Theodore.

He certainly loved everyone fussing over him.

Our Puppy Is A Monster
(He'll eat anything)

We were in the middle of doing a renovation to our house, we were adding a master bedroom on the upper (main floor), and we had the new bedroom finished before Barney passed away. Now we were adding hardwood floor to the rest of the house. Jim was doing the hardwood himself, and he had a little helper. Little did he know that while he was going ahead with placing the flooring and hammering it in. Theo was always just behind him chewing on a piece of hardwood that was lying on the floor ready to be installed. Of course Jim was not too happy of all the ruined pieces of wood that Theo decided were his.

He was terrible he had this thing about him; he always had to stick his nose in every ones butt. (he still does), we just can't get him to stop it. It gets really embarrassing, especially when people come to visit. When we do have company we hang on to him because we know what he's going to do, when he gets use to the company we let him go. Then he goes straight for their butt. Even us, of course while Jim was working on the floor it was one hand on the hammer and one hand waving behind him trying to shoo Theo away. He is 10 years old this year and still does it. He is really sneaky too.

At that time I had my office in my house, I was working on my computer, not knowing that he was anywhere in site. All of a sudden he jumps up at the front of my desk and slaps his two front paws up on the top of my desk as if to say "I'm here, play with me" I was so glad that I had my camera with me. You see I don't go anywhere without my camera, especially when there is a young beast in the house. I don't want to miss out on any of the hilarious memories.

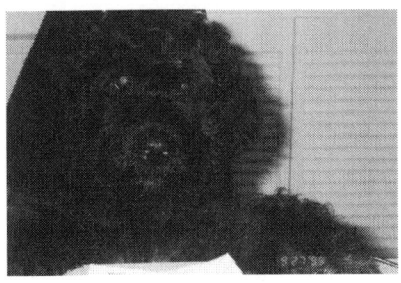

I'm lonely . . . what are you doing mom?

He also had a horrible habit of going through garbage cans when we weren't home. All the bathroom garbage cans had lids on them. They were the type you would step on a pedal to open. Well I guess either to get back at us for going out, or I don't know maybe he was just hungry, anyways he would knock over all the cans and strew garbage all over the place, what a mess, we would have to close the bathroom doors every time we went out. We had 3 bathrooms on the main floor and one on the lower floor. He would even go into Jim's office and go through that garbage can. Thankfully he didn't know how to open the cupboard under the kitchen sink. Again, still to this day he goes through the garbage cans, not as often though, only when he is really mad at us for going out.

One day while Jim was working in his office in the house, he noticed that Theo had been outside in the back yard for a long time, so he opened the door and called him. Theo came running from the hillside at the back of the yard, when he got inside he was running sideways and ran into the wall. Jim thought that was kind of weird, then he noticed that Theo seemed to be a little dizzy and couldn't stand straight. We figured he must have gotten into some type of weeds in the backyard, obviously something that wasn't good for anyone to eat. I'll bet he was hallucinating too; he was showing signs like he was high.

I decided to paint my crafts room, as I was rolling paint on the walls, Theo was helping himself to eating the paint out of the pan. I looked at him and he had white paint all over his face. We called the vet and he told us what to do, and to make sure he drank lots and lots of water. We knew then that nothing was safe around Theo, and to our amazement he never got sick from it. Just like Barney they both had a cast iron stomach.

Theo's New Friend

His name is Fonzie, you couldn't tell the two apart if you didn't know them, Fonzie is a year older than Theo and with birthdays only 1 week apart. They were like little children when his owner Monica and myself took them to the park to play, they haven't seen each other now probably for a couple of years, even though I keep in touch with the owners. Lives and situations change and people move and also we don't always have the time that we had before. My plan is to get them together soon again.

I met Monica just after Barney died, we were driving home one day and I spotted her and her puppy on the road. I told my husband to stop the car so I could go out and see the dog. First thing Fonzie did was jump on me and scratched me all the way down my leg. After that Monica and I became friends. When I informed her about Theo, she said great now we can take the dogs for walks together. It was easy at first. Fonzie was (and I say was because he has aged, like Theo) hyper and spunky, Monica says that he is still somewhat hyper and rambunctious especially when people come to visit, but toned down a lot. When the dogs first got together, They were so excited, they would jump all over each other and chase one another, it was hard to control them when they were so happy. We would laugh, after about 6 months Fonzie would get a little rough with Theo, and Theo would back off somewhat. He was a lot more hyper then Theo was and at times we would have to tell Fonzie to back off, I don't think Theo liked him so close all the time. Otherwise they were the best of friends, all you had to do was mention to each of them the other's name and their ears would perk up and they'd get excited.

People would spot them together and think they were brothers. At times I thought they looked like two bear cubs in the grass when they laid down to rest. Actually they could probably have scared someone if they had been stumbled upon and we weren't there.

Theo on left. . . . Fonzie on the right

Trying to train them was difficult

Theo and Fonzie had the same quirks, they both ate whatever they saw; they wanted all your attention and affection. They would nudge you at night time if they had to go out to the bathroom. They didn't like being alone, and they had the same weird sexual desires. It sounds weird doesn't it? It was hard to explain this when I mentioned to the vet that even though Theo had been neutered he still wanted to have sex, but not with human legs like a lot of puppies do, Theo never did that, oh no . . . . he wanted to have sex with cars!!!

With the back seat! His favorite and still to this date is a foam wedge that the small dogs use to climb up onto the bed with. Fonzie liked having sex with a blanket; he would roll it up and go at it. The vet said that it was normal, that they will still have the desire and don't understand it. I guess we just have to except that he will continue to do . . . IT . . . with abnormal items.

Theo going at it, with the foam wedge and Shadow looking on.

On one of my moms' visits to our place, we decided to take the dog to the provincial park just up the street from our house. So we loaded him in the vehicle and as my mom and I were getting our seatbelts on, the jeep started to rock sideways. I yelled out "I haven't even started the car yet what the heck is going on back there". My husband was in the driveway laughing, I then turned around and saw Theo straddled over the back seat and going at it with the seat. "Don't try to stop him" my husband yelled out, "you will upset him and you don't want him growling at you". How embarrassing that was, my mom thought it was hilarious. I'm just glad it was her in the vehicle not someone else. We had a good walk, I kept him on the leash on the roads and sidewalks and then off in the trails I take his leash off and let him go for a good run. On the way home you could tell he was tired, panting and just staring out the window . . . . Until we got about 1000 feet from the house, he was straddling the back seat again and going at it. My mom looked back at him and laughed, he in reply growled at her. Now that was funny, I guess he thought she was going to try to stop him. My mom said, "I don't think he wants me looking at him".

Back to Theo and Fonzie . . . . The dogs also loved to swim; they wouldn't have the title Water Dog if they didn't like the water. Trying to get them out of the water was a job.

Using one toy for them to fetch was like 2 children arguing over a toy, they would both run into the water after the toy, when one was closer to it, the other stopped but as he got to shore they fought over who got the toy. So from then on we brought down a toy for each, and then they decided they didn't want to fetch the toy anymore. Definitely stubborn dogs, if they didn't get their way then they wouldn't play. Sounds a lot like children.

WINTER FUN!

The dogs were crazy, snow, rain or shine, didn't matter, all that was on the agenda was play, play and more play. They sure kept us fit in exercise though. Anyone not in good health or physical condition, I would deter buying one of these breeds. They are not as hyper as a Border collie if they don't get exercised often enough, but they do have a lot of energy and want to be exercised or they will become fat and lazy.

Theo Needs A Live-In Companion

We had noticed a change in Theo every time we went out for a few hours, his disposition was completely different as from before we left. He would be panting, eyes bulging, and extremely hyper. Also he would get into anything available to his height. The garbage cans to search through garbage. Shoes to chew on, any of my figurines especially if they were made of wood, plants, he would chew on whatever caught his fancy. It was almost like he had panic attacks while we were out. Many times we said we wish we had a camera to record while we were gone to see exactly what he did. Once he even had a poop on our living room couch. (Barney had done the exact same thing) I couldn't believe it; it was like he was getting back at us for going out and leaving him alone. He was always a good dog for going outside to do his business; we never had trouble training him that way. So it was a shock to see what he had done. We figured it would be best not to stay out as long anymore, at least until he grew up. Little did we know that he would also take 7 years to grow up out of his puppy stage. So now I tell anyone that wants a Porty how long it takes for them to mature. That can also make a difference in the decision of owning this breed.

For Christmas we made plans with the rest of the family to spend it at a mountain resort, we figured we would spend about 3-4 days there, do some snow mobiling, etc. There were 15 of us plus 3 dogs Theo and my sisters dog Q and my brothers dog Rex. I was amazed at how well Theo and Rex got along; Rex is a Lasso Apso and pretty much the same age. Rex is a few months older; they played together so well that it was sad to split them up when it was time to leave. Although that gave me the push to get another dog for Theo, and maybe he would stop with the panic attacks when we went out. I always wanted a small lap dog anyways, so here was my opportunity (we would all around win). This was going to be Theodore's Christmas present (and mine).

The day after Christmas Jim and I went to the pet store hoping they would have some puppies, they actually had a few different breeds. The pups that caught our eye were Pekingese X Lasso Apso mix, although I think they got wrong information, they looked more like Pekingese X with King Charles. There were 6 tan/brown color and one black and white. I asked the clerk if the black and white belonged to the litter and she said yes he did, they were all so adorable, and if I could I would have taken them all.

Now I wanted a boy; that I knew, we spent at least 1 hour with them to see which one we would take, a couple of them were happy just sleeping, I picked up a couple of them to see how they reacted. The one we kept going back to was the black and white one. He was so adorable; he looked like Gizmo from the Gremlins movie. I picked him up and he snuggled under my chin and he went to sleep. I said this is the one, I have made up my mind I want him. Jim kept saying are you sure, I said yes, now we just have to make sure that he is a boy. It took a while for the girl to check; I couldn't tell at 8 weeks, she assured me he was a boy. Great, sold.

I had never had a lap dog before and always wanted one. So in reality I think we got the dog more for me than for Theo, at least Jim tells me so. I fell in love with him, I couldn't say enough about how cute he was. His bulging eyes and tiny body, he was just so adorable. When we brought him home the kids fell in love with him. We didn't know how Theodore would respond to a live in pal, but he really didn't have a choice, and in the end it was the best thing we ever did for Theo, as of the writing of this book, they have been together for 9 years and are inseparable.

We named him Shadow, we didn't just fumble across the name, it was actually quite appropriate . . . why? Because Shadow would follow

Theo everywhere he went . . . actually he still pretty much does. So it was appropriate to call them Theo and his Shadow. Shadow took to Theo immediately the first day we brought him home. Theo was not too sure about him; Shadow was tiny probably about 5 lbs. to Theo's 35 lbs. Of course Theo was, 18 months older than Shadow. It looked so cute seeing the two of them get closer and closer in becoming buddy's. Shadow definitely earned his name.

THEO AND HIS SHADOW

The first few nights were very difficult to sleep, we had a small carrying kennel for Shadow but he didn't want to sleep in it all night, he would cry half way through the night, he probably figured Theo wasn't in a cage so why should I be. Of course I felt bad for him and mainly wanted to get some sleep so I put him in bed with us, (I did it again) that's a big NO NO . . . . to this day he still comes up onto our bed and snuggles in under my arm and blanket. Although, I must say not in the summer time . . . too hot.

It took Theo about 10 days to get comfortable with Shadow, part of it may have been jealousy, he wasn't getting all of the attention anymore, and he had to share it. Shadow wanted to play all the time and Theo wasn't always interested. Theo was a good trainer for shadow, when we sent Theo out to the bathroom Shadow would follow, when I asked Theo to shake his paw for a treat Shadow would watch, and eventually follow suit. Taking them for walks was hilarious, Shadow would grab Theo's leash and pull on it. So that it looked like he was taking Theo for a walk, and he continuously did this during the walk. A few times Jim would let go of the leash because Shadow had control of it, and Theo didn't seem to mind. I really think what happened was Shadow slowly got control of Theo, because to date Shadow still seems to rule the roost when it comes to Theo. Theo lets Shadow do anything and get away with everything. For example Theo has a large pillow bed; Shadow has a small wooden frame bed, and every night, to no fail. Shadow is found sleeping in Theo's bed, and Theo will be lying on the floor beside his bed. Shadow looks lost in Theo's bed because of his size. We literally have to pick Shadow up and put him back in his own bed. If they are having dinner and Shadow decides he wants some of Theo's then Theo will back off and let him eat it. If Shadow decides he wants some of Theo (which is hilarious to watch) then Theo just sits still and lets Shadow have his way. Usually this happens after shadow has had a good and tasty dinner.

The two of them are so compatible; I don't know how they could go on without each other. When one goes to the vet the other gets so excited when he returns, then the full body sniffing begins and then they start to play. Sometimes they sleep together on Theo's bed, when one had surgery and came home the other would become mom or nurse to him. When Theo had surgery on his knee, he had his whole side and leg shaved. Shadow would go up to him and lick his wounded area, and then clean his face. The same happened when Shadow had surgery on both his front arms; Theo did much of the same thing. We really are worried when the time comes when one of them are not around anymore, not just because it would be like loosing one of our children but because it will hurt the other dog so deeply without his buddy around.

They play together all the time, sometimes Theo starts to agitate Shadow or the other way around and then the play fighting starts. When we are out for a walk on our property without a leash (25 acres) Shadow is the slow poke, he has to sniff everything in site. Sometimes we are 50-75`ahead of Shadow and realize he's not following us, so I'll look behind and yell out Shadow come on lets go. Then Theo will hide behind some weeds (he will actually lay on the ground) and get in attack mode, so that when Shadow gets within 10`of us then Theo lunges out at him as if to give him heck for being so slow

When Shadow was 3 months old he was having a lot of problems walking, he would fall over his front feet at times, and we could see his bold legs were giving him grief. So we brought him back to the vet, he said that he needed surgery on both front legs, and by doing this we would be giving him a better life. So we agreed he ended up having the bone in one front leg shortened and the other straightened. We called the pet store that we bought him through and told the owner what was going to happen. He offered to give us back our money or another dog. I said no, that's not what I want, by giving Shadow back, they would end up having him euthanized, I couldn't bare the thought of that, I was already in love with him. All I wanted was some help with the cost of the surgery, but if they weren't going to help then that was okay too. I would do anything for my Shadow. As it turned out they gave us back most of our money to help pay for his surgery. We were so grateful. We ended up as one of their best customers for all the things we purchased through their store including another dog later on.

The day came for Shadow's surgery, we were really nervous, he was in the veterinary hospital for about 3 days, and both front paws were completely shaved and had stitches all the way up both legs. He wasn't supposed to jump or run for about 1 week. Ya right, how am I supposed to stop that from happening when he lived with Theo? Mind you Theo was much gentler with him.

I bought a baby carrier so that we could still take him for walks with us without making him walk. When we went camping and I put this front carrier on me and put Shadow into it. I did get a lot of looks and of course I had to explain why I had my dog in it instead of having him walk.

Yes, he's my baby

The doctor assumed that shadow would have arthritis in his legs by the time he was 3 or 4 years old. He turned 9 in October and he still is full of spunk. Yes there are times that he just doesn't want to walk anymore and we have to carry him. Or a few times I have noticed him stumble over his front legs, and sometimes I can tell that he is in some pain. We have him on glucosamine to help his joints, and a few other things the vet has told us to give him. But all in all he is in great health considering.

It Feels Like we have 2 toddlers in the house

 I have always said that if I had to do life over again, I wouldn't have kids, I would just have dogs. They are easier to take care of, cheaper to raise, and you don't get the same back talk, or the phone calls from the school complaining about your child; Or the fights with neighbors'. Although . . . . after having 2 young dogs I might take that back. Theo being only 1 ½ years older than Shadow doesn't make him more mature. When the two of them start to play anything in their way would get pushed over. They were always finding new things to get into, and clever. i.e. I had a small carry kennel for Shadow in Jim's office. Shadow loved going into there for his naps. Theo had a larger crate and it was in my crafts room just down the hall. Well we found out that Shadow was a thief. Days would go by where by we would be complaining of missing items, one day I happened to look into Shadows crate and found Jim's watch, his pj's, my aerobics' bathing suit, and my bra and this would go on for a long time, he claimed what was easy for him to pick up; and hide it. Then one day I spotted Shadow walking down the hall with a yarn of wool from my crafts room. I yelled out "Hey you little bugger STOP right now . . . . He froze. I took it from him and put it back in my room and noticed the bag I had on my chair full of wool was scattered on the floor with strings of different colors going all over the place and they ended up in Theo's crate. I had started an afghan blanket and I left the crochet needle and the yarn that I was working with wrapped in the blanket. With Shadow pulling and playing with it he unraveled several rows of the blanket, and he tried to stuff it all in Theo's crate. I'm thinking to make it look like Theo had done this horrible mess.

Caught in the Act . . . . Bad Shadow

Ah yah . . . . , its like having small children again.

Sunbathing together

Shadow's bed

Afternoon nap together Theo too big for Shadow's bed

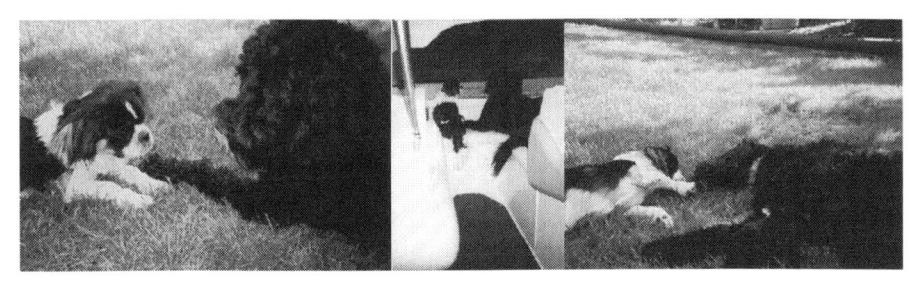

Best pals

Three Years Later . . . .

Dog #3 . . . It was early November of 2003, we were in the same pet store that we always shopped in. I was looking at the iguanas' when I heard Jim call my name. I went over to where he was, which was at the puppy window. He said to me . . . . "I probably am doing the wrong thing by calling you over here, but I thought you might want to see these puppies". Well, he knows how hard it is for me to say no to a puppy, so why really did he ask me over to look at them? My birthday was just around the corner, we talked about it for a short time, and yes he bought me a female shitzu/toy poodle for my birthday. She was a doll, I never had a female dog before so I thought it would be a nice change, she was all black with a little bit of white on her feet. While we were going over her paperwork etc. she climbed into my purse which was on the counter and went to sleep.

Princessa Comes Home

We wondered what the kids were going to say to a third dog in the house. I'm sure they would think that we were nuts. We probably were. When we got home I said guess where we were? We bought another dog! Daniel didn't believe me he thought I was joking, but when I showed her to him he said you guys are crazy, 3 dogs? When he got over the initial shock he played with her, he thought she was cute. Aaron fell in love with her. We called her Princessa Cessa for short, she was our little princess, and we never had a daughter so she fit right in. The first several nights were a real struggle to get some sleep, Shadow kept coming up onto our bed to sleep, and Cessa didn't want to sleep in Shadows kennel just like Shadow didn't want to when he first came home. So we brought her up to our bed, (I know another NO NO, can't stop now) but she slept with Jim because Shadow was jealous of her and I didn't want him to feel left out. She ended up becoming more of Jim's dog. This seems to happen a lot when a female dog comes into the family she seems to get closer to the male and vise versa with the male. We have noticed that with a lot of couples and their dogs.

It took some time but all three dogs eventually became close like brothers and sister. With Cessa being the female she eventually became like a mother hen. She mothered Theo and Shadow and as she got older she bossed them around. The funniest thing we ever saw was when she was lying on our bed and Theo came into the bedroom she barked and barked at him and he was almost terrified of her. It got to the point where he didn't want to enter the bedroom anymore unless Jim or I escorted him in. Boy she really has him wrapped around her finger, she's the boss alright.

After her 1st bath   1st Christmas   Theo sharing his bed

    She was about 1 year old and I noticed that she had drops of blood dropping on the floor. That's when I realized that she was having her period. I had never had a female dog before so this was all new to me. I had to get her little dog panties with liners. It sounded so silly to go to the dog store to buy these items but it was natural. Of course Theo and Shadow were all over her even though they had been fixed, they could sense something. Jim and I had talked about allowing Cessa to have 1 litter, I told him that I would take care of the puppies and I would sell them, and there was no way I would keep any of them because 3 dogs was enough.

    I put an ad in the paper looking for a stud, preferably a Lasso Apso or a purebred shitzu. I got an answer back from the owner of a Lasso but he was already 10 years old. The owner also said that he has been with a few females and nothing came of it. So I turned that one down. The only other one was the owner of a shitzu purebred. So I went to meet them and she informed me that every female her dog mates with gets pregnant within 1 week. So I set up a time to bring Cessa over. When that day came Cessa did not want to stay, the male was after her and she would hide behind me. I felt so bad leaving her with him but I didn't have a choice. I told the owner I was going to do some shopping and would be back. A couple of hours later I came back and she said that he finally got her and that I should know in a couple of weeks if it took, well I waited a month and nothing happened, she got her period again. So I called the owner and told her we would have to try it again. This time I left her there while I went to work. When I picked her up the breeder told me that he got her twice and that one should take.

Poor Cessa, I felt like I was farming her out to get pregnant. (I guess that was what I was really doing). Anyways, that one took.

Princessa Is Going To Be A Momma

Cessa was 18 months old when she had her pups. She weighed around 9-10 lbs when she got pregnant, she was a small dog and the stomach she was carrying was so low to the ground, I felt that she would have to pop soon because she was just too large for her size. (I believe it was around 3 months of pregnancy), I learnt as much as I could to help her through the birthing process if I needed to. I also took her to the vet for checks and then for an ultrasound I wanted to know how many pups there would be in case of problems. She was going to have 5 puppies; I was shocked, even the vet said that was a lot for her size. It was so cute seeing all the little puppies in her tummy.

One evening while Jim and I were watching tv, Cessa was acting strangely; she was carrying one of her stuffed animals around with her all evening. Then she jumped on the couch between us. I said Jim, this may be the night, she is not acting like herself. So we started to get prepared just in case. When we finally went to bed she wanted to sleep between our pillows, so I put a towel down and let her sleep on that. We watched a little tv until all of a sudden she let out this horrific screech. One of the sacks with a puppy in it was half way out. Jim and I both scrambled to get out of the bed to put her in a bed that I had made up for her for when she was ready to give birth. It had towels in it for the mess that we were going to encounter. While I gently picked her and the sack up to put in the bed she tried to run away. I got her on the floor and she tried to run under the bed with the sack still hanging out, We were nervous and had to try to calm her down, it was like she was running away from the pain, she would look down to see what was coming out of her and trying to get away from it. I helped by gradually pulling the puppy out and then I cleaned off its face and the rest of it. By the time the second one came she took over. Thank God! She was so perfect at cleaning them and of course she wanted to eat each of the placentas, I didn't know if she was supposed to do this or not. I was feeling ill watching this so I wrapped up the rest of them to through out. She started to give birth at 12:00 am and by 3:00am in the morning 4 were born.

I was glad that I had the ultrasound done because if I didn't then I would have thought that she was done. About an hour went by and we started to get worried, she would whimper but nothing would happen, I would massage her stomach and back to try to help but still nothing. So Jim made an emergency call to the vet around 4:00am, of course the answering service picked up, they made the call to the vet and he got online. He said that some times the last one can take a while. Give it another couple of hours, which we did. By 6:00am she was still not giving birth so we called the vet and said we have to bring her in. So he met us at the clinic at 7:00 on a Sunday morning. He tried to manually take the puppy, he got as far as getting one leg out and that was it. It was getting too much for Cessa, I was so afraid for her; I didn't want her to die from all the pain and stress. So the vet did a C-Section on her, there was the last puppy, but sadly he was stillborn. The vets' helper gave me the puppy in a towel and said start rubbing vigorously at its heart, tummy back, etc. which I did for 15 minutes hoping I could revive it. But nothing happened. He was the largest of the 5 pups. It was a sad day, then I would look over at the other 4 puppies that we brought with us, they were under a heat lamp and I was so proud of Cessa for bringing those 4 beautiful puppies into this world. I just hoped that she would be okay after all she went through.

Not long after her surgery did she wake up and she was put in the bed with her surviving puppies, she immediately started to clean and feed them. She was going to be a good mother. A few hours after arrival we took her and the puppies' home to recuperate. While she was in surgery I had asked the vet to spade her also. I wouldn't put her through that again. No Way!

She had 1 girl and 4 boys minus the one that was stillborn. They were so sweet, the whole birthing process was such an experience for us to be able to witness and be there with her to help. This was something we will never forget.

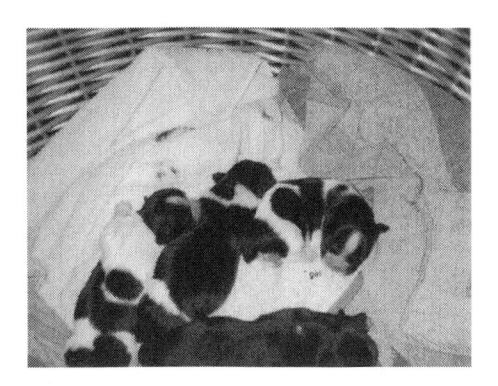

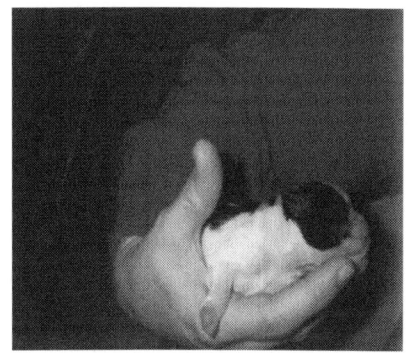

Day 1—February 6 2005

Eight Dogs in the house

The first month went by not too bad; I had set up a fenced area in the house for mom and the pup's. Poor Theo and Shadow, they were very curious with the puppies, whenever they went to the pup's bed to sniff, Cessa would run over to her babies and growl at either Theo or Shadow, she was so possessive over her new ones, it was actually adorable. Even if I decided to take one or several of them and just hold them on the couch, she would follow me and sit beside me, I'm sure she trusted me but neither Jim nor I could be alone with the pups without her being there with us.

Towards the 5th week we noticed that Cessa was slowly weaning the babies, and they didn't like that, several times throughout the night she decided she wanted to sleep with us again on the bed and you could hear the puppies crying . . . . They were hungry; several times I would bring her back to them. I felt like I was their mom and I was getting up several times a night for feedings, and I had to get up early for work. It was as if Cessa was saying mom please take over for me, I'm exhausted. At six weeks I put an ad in the paper for the puppies so that they could go to their new homes at 8 weeks. I gave one to my sister for her 50th Birthday. She got to pick which ever one she wanted. The only female went to the Breeder as payment. So that was two spoken for, I had just 2 left. The sale I was going to make on these two was not even going to cover the vet costs for the C-Section. No one counted on that but it didn't matter. There was one black with a white daisy face left and another with patches of white and black.

Our 2ND Generation Kids

It was the last 2 weeks before the pups were to be in their permanent homes. Daniel our youngest 16 years at the time asked if he could keep one. I looked at him and said are you crazy? 3 dogs is a lot, 4 would be incomprehensible. Daniel kept at me for a week; he said that if he could keep one, the one he wanted was the runt of the litter, all black with the daisy face. He had a few problems i.e. hernia in his lower stomach that we had operated on and his nostrils seemed to be pinched, so when he ate he choked, the vet said that would go away with age. Daniel really put the pressure on as more people came to see the two pups. I said Daniel I have enough work with the 3 dogs. He said "well it would be my dog, I would walk him and feed him and when I get a job I will pay for everything that he needs". It sounded good, but I wasn't ready to believe him. One evening a mother and her toddler came to look at the pups, Daniel kept saying I hope they don't take the black one. He had already named it Ozzie. They played with the two and couldn't make up their minds. In my heart I was also hoping they didn't take the black one. She ended up choosing the black and white. So Ozzie was the only one left. I slept on the idea for a few nights and had several conversations with Jim about it. Jim said "you know Daniel won't keep up with the duties of taking care of a dog, and are you ready to take care of 4 dogs when Daniel looses interest"? Well Ozzie had been with us already 8 weeks, and he was Cessa's son, it would be so nice for Cessa to have one of her sons live with her. (Man I was a sucker)

So we gave in, we told Daniel "yes you can keep him . . . . BUT!! You are his owner, which means you feed him walk him, clean up the yard after him, and when you get a job, you pay for his vet checks, shots, grooming, food, etc." He agreed to it . . . . But I knew it wouldn't last. It lasted about 1 month, slowly I was doing everything for Ozzie that Daniel should be doing. He didn't even want to sleep in Daniel's bedroom, because his mom slept with us. Cessa was so good to him, the relationship today still continues as a mom and son. She gives into him when he wants something she has, she sleeps next to him, they play together, fight together, and the two of them are as tight together as Theo and Shadow are. This is actually just perfect.

Mom and son   *Mom and two sons*

One day we were coming home and Ozzie came running straight to me and ignored Daniel. Daniel said you stole him from me he doesn't come to me anymore. I said "well maybe because he knows that I'm the one that spends the time with him and feeds him and bathes him etc". So from then on Daniel knew he was fighting a lost battle, Ozzie would never look to him as his owner. He belonged to his mom. Of course Daniel loves him like no other.

Today the dogs are one big happy family, when one goes to the vet the others are so excited to see him or her come back home. Princessa still gets to see one of her other son's periodically, the one I gave to my sister. His name is Archie, mom doesn't seem to remember him anymore as her son, but they all do get excited to see each other. I also think Archie knows that this is his birth home. My sister says that when they get to a certain street before our house Archie gets excited.

Theodore the Porty turned 10 in June. Shadow the Pek X turned 9 in October, Princessa the shitzu (mom) turned 6 in September, and Ozzie the shitzu (son) was 4 in February. This little family has turned out better than I ever thought. The biggest problem we will have will be as we slowly start loosing them, it will literally break our hearts, and these dogs are our kids, *"Our 2nd Generation Kids".*

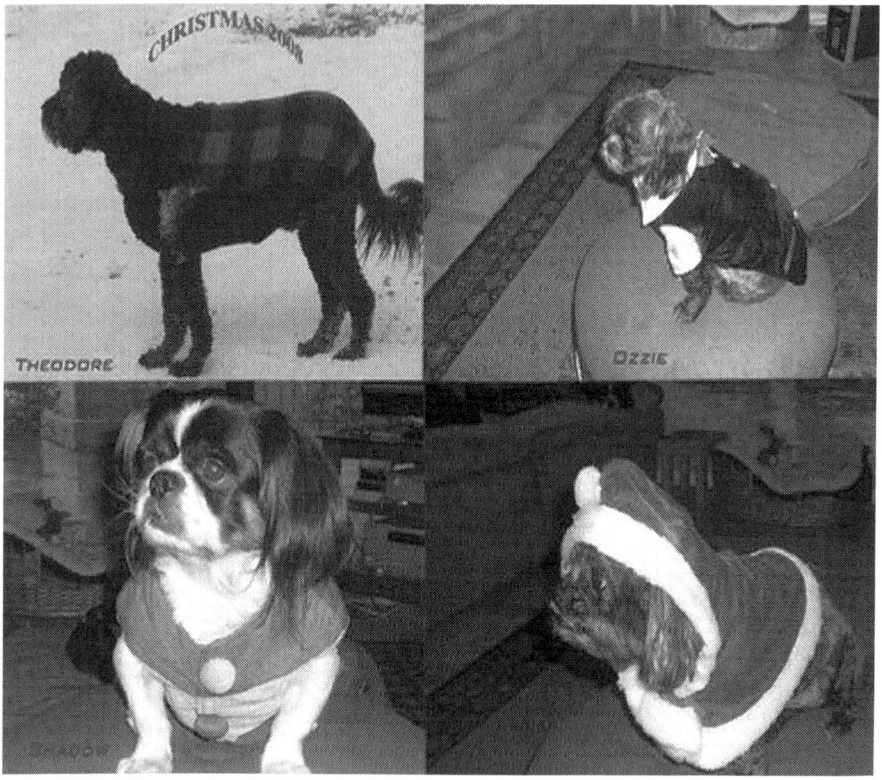
CHRISTMAS
THEODORE
OZZIE
SHADOW

So it all started with Theodore's anxiety when he was left home alone, and his need for a companion. Who knew that 1 dog would turn into 4. When Jim hears me say oh I'd love to have a pug. He right away say's "NO WAY!! You get one more dog and I move out!" So I guess I will have to wait to get the pug . . . . maybe

These guys have made our lives so fulfilling, yes times we wondered what we had gotten into with 4 dogs. They would ruin things in the house or the barking would drive me crazy when they spot a deer in the backyard, or a squirrel. Or times that we wanted to spend the night at friends and none of the kids could come back home and stay the night. It really was like having small children again, but we coped. We love them to death and wouldn't have it any other way.

So for those of you that want to get a Portuguese Water dog, really make sure you have a lot of time to spend with him/her and don't mind living with a puppy for 7 years. Also accept that you may have to get a companion for the Porty and that could lead to more. Especially if you're a real animal lover like me . . . and a sucker.

As for Barney, we will never forget him he will always be in our hearts, I have beautiful pictures of him in our bedroom and we think of him a lot, but these guys have truly helped take the pain away of loosing Barney.

Acknowledgements

I have a lot of people to Thank for the encouragement in the writing of this book. Dr. E Kaplan our veterinarian in Lake Country B.C. for giving Barney an extra 2 years of life, and just as importantly he gave us another 2 years with Barney. He continues to be the vet for our dogs today. My husband, for encouraging me to write this book. My kids for having an interest in it. My mother for showing so much excitement while reading the drafts. I have wanted to right this book for a few years now, but never had the time nor the discipline. I was recently in a car accident so it has given me the time to put my best effort into this. Not many people know about the Portuguese water dog, and I thought this would be a great way to let people know what they are about to embark upon if they do want one for a pet. But also how beautiful they are. Yes there were times we wished we didn't have him, but more than not, we loved him, more than we ever thought we could. Same goes for the rest of the dogs. They are part of our family and we wouldn't want it any other way.

References from:
www.canadasguidetodogs.com/ortugesewater.htm

The unknown Author for the Rainbow Bridge Poem, I shed a lot of tears reading that poem but it also gave me happy and relieved thoughts of Barney.

The biggest Thanks of All are to all of our dogs, because without them there would be no book.

Thank You: Barney, Theodore, Shadow, Princessa and Ozzie.

Printed in Great Britain
by Amazon.co.uk, Ltd.,
Marston Gate.